Dunstanburgh Castle

NORTHUMBERLAND

HENRY SUMMERSON   MA, PhD, FSA, FRHS

Dunstanburgh Castle is set majestically on a coastal headland, in a region historically remote and difficult of access. Beneath its walls, stormy seas pound the rocky shoreline. Screams of seabirds echo eerily under its cliffs. Built on the grandest possible scale in the years after 1313 by Thomas Earl of Lancaster, the castle was later much altered by John of Gaunt in the 1380s. As a Lancastrian stronghold, it played a brief but important role in the Wars of the Roses. But during the sixteenth century it fell increasingly into decay and, by the time of the death of Elizabeth I in 1603, had become militarily redundant.

ENGLISH HERITAGE · LONDON

Contents

Bibliographical acknowledgements
Nearly all the documentary sources on
which this handbook is based were
transcribed from Public Records by Dr
Eric Cambridge, to whose labours the
present writer is heavily indebted.
The fullest account of Dunstanburgh and
its surroundings is still that contained in a
A History of Northumberland Vol. II, ed E
Bateson (Newcastle upon Tyne, 1895).
Photographs of the site unless otherwise
captioned, are from the English Heritage
Photo Library. The picture at the top of
page 13 is by the author.

Published by English Heritage,
23 Savile Row, London W1S 2ET
Copyright © English Heritage 1993
First published 1993, reprinted 1995, 1997, 2000, 2002
Printed in England by Westerham Press C80 12/02
ISBN 1 85074 350 9

Introduction

Romantic view of Dunstanburgh Castle, engraved in about 1825 from a drawing by Richardson. The building on the extreme right is no longer visible

The Site

The magnificent setting of Dunstanburgh Castle has long been admired by visitors. Eighteenth and nineteenth-century descriptions of the site are full of appreciative references to the 'abrupt frightful precipices on the east and north', to the 'noble though tremendous' breaking of the waves and the sound of the sea, and to the 'supreme grandeur of the scene'.

It says a great deal for their architectural quality and interest that the ruins actually enhance views so richly endowed by nature. Seen in this light, it was fortunate for Dunstanburgh that its castle should have been a product of the greatest age of English castle-building. For, apart from fragments of pottery from a settlement in the second century AD, there is no evidence for fortification here until Thomas of Lancaster started to build his castle in 1313.

This handbook departs from English Heritage's usual format, in that it is presented as a single narrative, without the conventional distinction between description and history. Instead, a historical introduction, explaining the origins and purpose of the castle, leads straight into a guided tour of the buildings, during which the use and development of the fabric are explained as seems necessary. History and architectural description are thus run together. You may prefer to start with the tour, and read about Dunstanburgh's early days later. But whatever your approach, please bear in mind that the castle, as you now see it, is a monument, a structure frozen in time, preserved in the condition in which it came into the keeping of H M Office of Works over sixty years ago. Walls and buildings which look fragile and insecure today will, as far as modern technology can achieve it, continue to look fragile and insecure in exactly the same way from here to eternity.

In being so resistant to alteration, the present-day castle differs greatly from the castle as it was in the past. This applies even to the fairly recent past, while in the days when it was in use as a working building, Dunstanburgh was in a state of continuous change, even if that change was all too often barely distinguishable from decay. Most of the evidence for the condition and design of the medieval castle comes either from warnings that parts of the fabric were about to fall down, or from payments for repairs after they had actually done so. On one occasion, as we shall see later, the whole lay-out of the castle was radically modified. There was nothing fossilised about Dunstanburgh in the Middle Ages.

Thomas of Lancaster and his Castle

You may have wondered as you came here why there should be a castle at Dunstanburgh at all. The site itself may be supremely defensible, but what besides itself does the castle actually serve to defend? Many castles were built to control roads or river crossings, to hold down conquered territory or to stabilise a new frontier. But the Anglo-Scottish border lies over 25 miles (40km) to the north, and the castle was built long after Northumberland had become inseparably attached to the English kingdom. The region's main north-to-south road, moreover, ran some way to the west, and there was no river crossing for the castle to dominate. Dunstanburgh Castle must therefore be explained, not so much by its position, as by the politics and personality of its builder, Thomas Earl of Lancaster, and by the circumstances of the time when he built it.

Dunstanburgh was part of the barony of Embleton. Neither Odard of Bamburgh and his descendants, a family of purely local importance who held that lordship from the early twelfth century until the middle of the thirteenth, nor the celebrated Simon de Montfort, who acquired it in 1255 from the heiress in whom Odard's line came to an end, thought it necessary to build a stronghold here. But by the early fourteenth century, when Thomas of Lancaster was Lord of Embleton (it had been given to his father Edmund by Henry III after Simon de Montfort was killed in the Battle of Evesham in 1265), things were different. The year 1296, when Thomas succeeded his father as Earl of Lancaster, also saw the beginnings of centuries of Anglo-Scottish conflict. At first the English armies, which had invaded Scotland under the direction of Edward I (1272-1307), usually held the upper hand. But after Edward's death that initiative was slowly lost.

The obsessive devotion shown by the new king, Edward II, for his homosexual lover, the deplorable Piers Gavaston, soon put him at loggerheads with the barons, who resented the extent to which the favourite monopolised the king's favour and patronage. His wealth and standing made Thomas of Lancaster the natural

Edward II from the effigy on his tomb (Gloucester Cathedral)

leader of the barons, and it was under his direction that Gavaston was finally judicially murdered in June 1312. In that same year the Scots, who had been largely undisturbed while the English king and his opponents settled their differences, and had taken advantage of this to recover lost ground in Scotland itself, now began a series of devastating raids into the north of England. The background to the building of Dunstanburgh Castle was one of political crisis and Scottish invasion.

Edward II never forgave Lancaster for his part in Gavaston's death, and the deed was followed by nearly eighteen months of tension bordering on civil war. Only in October 1313 did the earl and his accomplices receive a formal pardon, and by then work on Dunstanburgh had been in progress for some eight months. At a time when he was entirely unwelcome at court, Lancaster might well have felt the need for a powerful fortress as far away as possible from his angry king. In providing himself with one, he may in the process

have tried to set himself up in competition with the king in Northumberland, even though the resources of the barony of Embleton were barely sufficient for the support of a major castle, and were certainly not enough to pay for its construction, which was effectively subsidised from Lancaster's estates elsewhere.

It has been generally assumed that the name Dunstanburgh, which can be translated from Old English as 'the fort by the hill-rock', shows that the defensive possibilities of the castle's position were appreciated in the Anglo-Saxon period. But not only has archaeological research failed to provide any evidence for the occupation of the site between the second century and the fourteenth, but the name itself is unrecorded before 1313, when name and castle appear for the first time simultaneously. The neighbouring village of Dunstan, on the other hand, is several times mentioned in thirteenth-century documents. It seems likely, therefore, that the name Dunstanburgh was an artificial one, specially devised for the castle, with the word 'burgh' being deliberately tacked on to the place-name Dunstan in order to suggest comparisons with the king's castle at Bamburgh, some ten miles (16km) to the north on the same coastline.

In fact, at the time when Dunstanburgh was being built, Bamburgh was only indirectly a royal castle, since Edward I had entrusted it to Isabel de Vescy, the widow of a former lord of Alnwick, who neglected to keep it in repair. Dunstanburgh, built on similar lines to Bamburgh, may therefore have also been intended to serve as a hint to Edward II – on a very large scale – of his responsibilities in the north. It is likely enough that Lancaster, who seems to have had all the psychological penetration of a rhinoceros, never understood the extent to which Edward was outraged by

Medieval building works. A manuscript in John Rylands Library, Manchester

Gavaston's death, and did not expect the king to continue to bear a grudge against him for it. He would have hoped for a reconciliation much quicker and more sincere than actually occurred, after which the king and his barons, in unity, would at long last tackle the problem of the Scots. Dunstanburgh could thus be additionally seen as a massive reminder to Edward II that this, the defence of his realm against invasion, was what he should be attending to, instead of engaging in bitter quarrels with most of the English nobility, and also as a sign of Lancaster's own commitment to that cause.

Early in August 1315 Lancaster was given the command of all the king's forces in the north of England, and very soon afterwards, on 28 August, he received a licence to crenellate at Dunstanburgh. Such a licence conferred not so much formal permission to construct a fortress – that would have been pointless in this case, when work had been in progress for well over two years; rather it constituted the king's acknowledgement of the lawfulness of the castle's existence. Although relations between king and earl were hardly less strained afterwards than they had been before, at least Lancaster could now feel that Edward II had given his approval to this magnificent new stronghold.

It has been suggested that the wide open spaces within the castle are due to its having never been finished. However, it was regarded as a working fortress by 1319, when it had a janitor and a constable (a commanding officer), together with a garrison of foot-soldiers and mounted men-at-arms, and when the rebellious barons decided to flee to Dunstanburgh in 1322, it seems unlikely that they expected to find themselves in a builder's yard when they arrived there. There may well have been buildings still to be completed when Lancaster was executed in that year (see Biographical Note on page 34) – the Lilburn Tower near the north-west corner of the castle was one of them, as we shall see – but not to such an extent as would affect the castle's overall design. Lancaster, who was quite prepared to borrow money when his own supplies ran short, would certainly have been anxious to complete Dunstanburgh as quickly as possible, and although a castle constructed on such a scale could hardly have been habitable by the time the licence to crenellate was given, it may well have been defensible surprisingly quickly afterwards.

There were certainly many in the region who would have welcomed the earl's presence in strength in the borders, and wanted him to make all possible haste to consolidate it. Several of monasteries of the region, including Tynemouth Priory and Newminster and Alnwick Abbeys, showed how much they valued Lancaster's establishing himself at Dunstanburgh by providing horses and oxen to carry materials when building was in progress. One of the cart-horses was in fact intercepted and carried off by the Scots, an episode which shows how badly these religious houses needed the protection a great lord such as Lancaster could provide. And that protection would certainly have been appreciated by the earl's own tenants as well.

The immense enclosure within the castle walls – eleven acres (nearly 4.5ha), more than any other castle in Northumberland – far from being evidence for the castle's completeness, was actually essential to its proper functioning. It could receive the Earl of Lancaster and his retinue if they chose to take refuge there. And it would also provide a place of safety for the earl's tenants, with their goods and livestock, in times of danger. When the castle was being built that danger was already pressing. The set of accounts that record the earliest building works at Dunstanburgh also record that getting in the harvest at Stamford, only

Prisoners and livestock being driven away by soldiers (British Library)

2½ miles (4km) to the west, had been disturbed by the Scots.

Lancaster was not in fact a considerate landlord, and the property he would have been most concerned about was certainly his own – he is recorded as growing corn, barley, oats and hay, and as rearing horses, oxen and pigs, as well as owning fisheries and mills, on his Northumberland estates. But it was also in his interest to defend the people of the surrounding villages, who could hardly have paid him their rents and other dues if all their possessions were forever being stolen or burnt. Constructing a castle might seem an expensive way of providing such a defence, even though the earl, as we have already seen, probably had additional motives for building one at Dunstanburgh. But Lancaster was a typical medieval aristocrat.

Not only did he give little thought to matters of cost, but he wished the results of his expenditure to be as conspicuous as possible. In fact he was rather untypical among his contemporaries in his belief in the importance and desirability of castles – he financed major works on at least five others – but it was inevitable that once he had decided to build at Dunstanburgh, he should have done so on a grand scale.

Other lords would eventually see to their own defence by building those simple and solid tower-houses which nowadays seem such a characteristic feature of the English border counties. But a magnate like the Earl of Lancaster did not think in terms of mere usefulness, even though a structure on the scale of Dunstanburgh Castle was arguably out of all proportion to any purely military purposes it might serve. For a lord of his greatness something special was required.

Bird's-eye view of Dunstanburgh Castle

Lilburn Tower
A watchtower and a residence for soldiers, with a postern at its foot, the early fourteenth-century Lilburn Tower dominates the approaches to the castle from the north-west. Its first-floor living quarters had direct access to the wall walk.

Sea cliff Originally there was a wall along the north side of the castle, but today the only defences here are natural ones, in the shape of a precipitous cliff face, where Kittiwakes and other seabirds breed.

Mantlet The wall built in the early 1380s to create a new inner ward behind Thomas of Lancaster's Gatehouse

Inner Ward
The courtyard of the inner castle, containing lodgings, an oven, a well, and other buildings intended to meet the garrison's everyday needs.

West Curtain Wall
The west wall ran along the edge of a steep incline. The ruined turret could have provided lateral fire, and also served as a look-out post.

John of Gaunt's gatehouse
Built in the early 1380s to provide a more conventional but still very heavily defended entrance to the castle. It was reached by a passage-way between a flanking wall and the west wall of the castle.

Flanking Wall Built in the early 1380s to control the approaches to John of Gaunt's gatehouse.

Thomas of Lancaster's Gatehouse A majestic early fourteenth-century gatehouse, originally dominated by four towers. In the late 1380s it was succeeded as the principal entrance to the castle by John of Gaunt's gatehouse, and became the castle keep instead.

Outer Ward The open expanses of the outer ward provided space for refugees and their livestock from the countryside around at times of Scottish raids. They also contained barns for storing grain and fodder, and an enclosure which was probably a vegetable garden in the Middle Ages. Female Eider Ducks often nest in the long grass.

East Curtain Wall The east wall faced the rocky foreshore, which itself formed part of the defences. The three garderobes along the wall were probably intended for the use of fugitives from the local villages, whose inhabitants may well have built this wall in the first place.

Postern Gate A small postern in the wall gave access to the foreshore and coast.

Egyncleugh Tower An important tower which commanded the 'clough', or ravine, under its east wall, and probably housed members of the garrison. On its south side a gateway, and a drawbridge spanning the moat, provided access to the coast and the little port.

South Curtain Tower The south wall protected the most vulnerable, and most heavily defended, side of the castle. This small turret supplied flanking fire along the wall.

Constable's Tower The residence of the castle's commanding officer, with a complex of buildings behind for his own use and that of his staff. The quality of the stonework is very high, and the finish of the windows and fireplaces show the importance given to basic comfort.

Illustration drawn by Terry Ball

Tour of the Castle

The early fourteenth-century gatehouse at Dunstanburgh Castle

The First Gatehouse

To start your tour, and also to take the full measure of the remarkable building which Thomas of Lancaster commissioned, you should go back now through the entrance in the south wall. To the west lie the level and fertile lands of the Barony of Embleton which the castle dominated and protected. And in front of you stands the great gatehouse which was at the centre of that castle's defences. Thomas of Lancaster was the richest man in England after the king, with an estimated yearly income of over £11 000. Architecture was an expensive commodity, but he could afford the best, which meant above all a gatehouse in the latest fashion, of the sort developed in Edward I's castles in Wales – there are close similarities between Dunstanburgh and Harlech, where too the gatehouse was the key to the defences. Both the gatehouse itself, as it survives today, and the building accounts for its construction, show that the earl spared no expense.

The mason in charge of the works, one Master Elias (he may have been identical with the Elias de Burton recorded earlier as working at Conwy in North Wales), was paid £280, a colossal sum at a time when agricultural labourers were earning about 1½d a day. Some £168 were spent on the first year's works, but the final cost was certainly a lot higher. As well as coals from Newcastle, Lancaster bought boards from the Baltic and iron from Spain. Much of the materials used would, of course, have been local in origin. Details of later repairs show that sand and lime could have been obtained from Craster, just to the south of the castle, and timber from the earl's estate at Shipley, north-west of Alnwick. But that did not mean

Medieval stonemason, from a carved fragment in the Yorkshire Museum

they were in any way deficient. The ashlar – cut stone – in which Lancaster's works were carried out certainly came from a quarry nearby, but was of the finest quality.

The gatehouse which Master Elias built for Thomas of Lancaster is impressive today, but, when newly finished, must have been both astonishing and intimidating. Looking at the front of the two great D-shaped projections which form its base, you can still see much of the ground floor and the two floors above it. Over these there was a smaller third floor whose roof supported a parapet-walk across the entrance – this could have served both as a look-out post and as a vantage-point from which to shoot arrows at any enemy who came within range. And on either side of this parapet, the curved projections at the front of the gatehouse were continued up for another two storeys as free-standing towers, completed by flat walls at the back.

Nor was this all, because on their inner sides these towers had additional turrets attached – as you can still see on the tower on the gatehouse's west side – which went even higher than the towers of which they formed part. From the summit of the western turret it is possible to see the top of the keep of Warkworth Castle some ten miles (16km) to the south, suggesting that these pinnacles were used for signalling as well as for reconnaissance, defence and defiance. And there were also tall towers at the north-east and north-west corners of the gatehouse. The lie of the land, and a ditch dug on the castle's west side to prevent its being attacked from that direction, meant that Dunstanburgh could really only be approached from the south. So once Thomas of Lancaster's works were completed, any marauding Scots coming up the causeway from the direction of Craster would have been confronted by a daunting array of walls

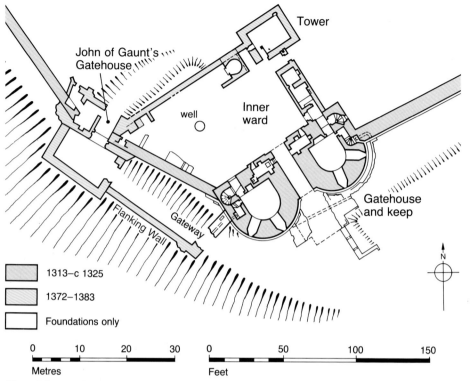

Plan of first gatehouse with, on the left, John of Gaunt's gatehouse

and turrets which were intended to rise to at least 80 feet (24m) above the ground.

Not that such attackers would have found it easy even to get as far as the gate, for quite apart from the danger of being shot from the parapet above, they would also have had to negotiate the forebuilding, a structure in front of the gatehouse intended to provide an additional obstacle for besiegers before they reached the gate, and there would certainly have been a pair of strong wooden gates at the front of the arch as well. The forebuilding has long since disappeared, while the gate archway has changed shape in recent times. Originally it was semi-circular and was still shown as such in a drawing of the 1850s. But it was also shown then as being propped up,

which explains why, at some time during the next fifteen years, its owner rebuilt it with the pointed arch we see today.

However, there is nothing to suggest that the inside of the gate passage has ever been seriously altered. As you go in through it, notice the mason's marks on the ribs of the vault. Some identical marks can be seen at Alnwick Castle, showing that the same craftsmen worked on both fortresses. Turn right on the other side of the gate passage – which was once also protected by a portcullis, whose grooves you can still see – and go into the first doorway on the right, that of a porter's lodge. There are two of these, one on each side of the gate. That to the west is not open to the public. But you can enter the other through a door which seems at some

From a distance Dunstanburgh gave a formidable impression to a would-be attacker

time to have been forced through the wall at the point where it was originally pierced by a narrow window (as is still the case with the chamber opposite).

The disappearance of its window makes this porter's lodge seem even barer than it was originally. Apart from the fireplace in the north wall, there is nothing to suggest that much thought was given to the comfort of its occupant, it is just a well-made but very plain rectangular room, with two deep recesses cut in its walls for storage. Even when the window still existed it cannot have let much light in, especially during the winter months, and the porter must often have had to use candles and lanterns to relieve the gloom of his lodging. The chamber on the other side has a cell underneath its floor. This may have been the cellar mentioned in a mid-fourteenth-century account, but it could also have been a prison, whose occupants must therefore have been confined in a darkness even greater than that of their gaoler above.

On coming out again, look at the wall

Unwelcoming porter. A medieval manuscript in the Bibliotheque de l'Arsenal, Paris

above, where you can see on each side of the central archway a semi-octagonal attachment looking rather like a rook on a chessboard. These are outlets for the smoke from the fireplaces in the porter's lodges (they are probably also the product of some comparatively recent restorer's antiquarian imagination, since they do not appear in eighteenth and nineteenth-century drawings and photographs). Continue along the wall to the next doorway and enter. Ignore for the moment the stair to the left which climbs to the floors above, peer into the garderobe, or privy, in the next doorway to the left, and then pause to view the large semi-circular chamber set in the gatehouse's ground floor.

As with the porters' lodges, there are two such chambers, identical with one another, one on each side of the gate passage. Both are worth looking at, though this guide will keep to the eastern side which is better preserved. The chamber would have been a guardroom, and we can imagine members of the garrison gathering in here while they waited for the call to go on duty, warming their hands at the fireplace in the north wall, and occasionally going to the deeply recessed arrow-slit windows to look at the weather or keep an eye out for enemy activity. Notice that one of these windows looks to the left and the other straight ahead. There is no window to the right because its outlook would have been blocked by the forebuilding in front of the gate.

The ground-floor rooms could have been used for fighting, by men firing arrows and bolts out of the slit windows, but that was not their principal employment. To see something of the way the gatehouse functioned defensively, you need now to go up the spiral staircase at the entrance to the guardroom to the floors above (originally it also served the tower at the north-east corner of the

gatehouse). The first floor served both domestic and military purposes. On each side of the gatehouse there was a large room above the guardroom below, with a third room between them over the gate passage. The outer chambers were clearly at least partly residential, judging by the fireplace in the east wall of the room nearest the stair and by the fine, deeply recessed windows, and may have housed leading members of the garrison. There is a little room off the south-west corner of the central chamber. Its garderobe shute shows that it was intended for the convenience of the garrison, but a loop in the south wall indicates that it would have been an observation post also.

In fact the whole of the central chamber seems to have been intended to serve military purposes, and when the castle was threatened with attack, its defence was probably directed from this room. It was here that the portcullis was lowered and raised – it is another sign of the overall high architectural standard that the portcullis groove was notably well and cleanly cut. It also has two floor-level holes at the front. These could have been used for observation, or for pouring down water, should an enemy set fire to the wooden gates below, or simply for shooting missiles at attackers.

If you continue up the spiral stairs, you will get fine views in all directions and also some idea of the lay-out of the rest of the gatehouse, even when the floors and much of the walls have disappeared. The second floor was basically a single long chamber, divided into three by wooden screens, and lit by windows to north and south – an eighteenth-century drawing shows two large windows in the north wall, set in stonework which has since collapsed. In the middle of this storey was the hall, where the garrison would have eaten, with a service area to the west of it and a chamber to the east. If Thomas of

Remains of the gatehouse's west tower, with a turret attached to its inner side. Beyond it are the lands of the Barony of Embleton, for which it was a refuge

Lancaster ever visited Dunstanburgh, the latter was probably the room he occupied.

The broad semi-circular arch above the south-facing second floor window was placed there to support the weight of the tower which rose above the height of the gatehouse proper. Since it would have been under the rear of that heightening, you can see how shallow those vertical exteriors were in comparison with the projection beneath them. Little of that tower survives, but if you look across to the remains of the west tower you can see the doorway by which it was entered from the parapet-walk which ran across the front of the gatehouse – the top of the doorway is carved in the 'shoulder headed' pattern characteristic of the years around 1300. And this is also the best place to see how cleverly its turret has been built on to the side of that tower and how neatly it is supported by its base of corbels (supporting stone brackets). Even at this great height, the ashlar blocks used are as well shaped as those at ground level. Scaffolding is known to have been used in the building of the gatehouse, and there was probably some sort of lifting device as well. Looking further across to the right, you can also see the base of the tower which stood at the opposite corner of the west side of the gatehouse.

John of Gaunt's Gatehouse

It is one of Dunstanburgh's peculiarities

The Kings of England and Scotland make a truce. Here Edward III shakes the hand of David II after the Treaty of Berwick in 1357 (British Library)

that it acquired a second gatehouse, when late in the fourteenth century it was radically re-ordered in such a way as to give it something much more like a castle's conventional layout, with an inner and an outer ward. Henry Duke of Lancaster, the nephew of Thomas who first built the castle, died without a male heir in 1361, and his only child was a daughter, Blanche. She married John of Gaunt, the third son of Edward III (1327-1377), who thus became Duke of Lancaster in the right of his wife, and so lord of Dunstanburgh (see Biographical Notes). Duke John was often engaged in northern affairs, especially when Anglo-Scottish relations, always tense, deteriorated badly in the late 1370s. Open war did not come until 1384, but the lords of the north of England knew it was imminent, and set their castles in order in preparation for it.

Lords and their retinue. A fourteenth-century manuscript in the British Library

The approach to John of Gaunt's gatehouse. On the left are foundations of a wall flanking the path. On the right is the base of a wall on which an outer gate hung.

Dunstanburgh is rarely mentioned in the records which survive from the period between the 1320s and the 1380s, but during the outbreak of Anglo-Scottish hostilities in the 1340s (which culminated in the defeat of the Scots at Neville's Cross in 1346) it is known to have fulfilled one of its original functions, by acting as a refuge, a subsequent account referring to 'chattels saved in the castle from the attack of the Scots'. But as a rule little can be said about it, except that now and again instructions were given that repairs be made to the castle, or accounts presented showing that such repairs had been duly carried out. John of Gaunt had ordered such works in 1372. He may have been alarmed by the castle's physical condition. Perhaps, too, as he became increasingly involved in the affairs of the north, he wanted a stronghold of his own which could counterbalance the great fortresses of his Percy rivals at Warkworth and Alnwick. But the measures he took a few years afterwards show that, as well as wanting to make Dunstanburgh an effective base for his own local authority, he was also dissatisfied with the castle's layout.

The fact that the early fourteenth-century gatehouse, in its position at the very centre of the castle's defences, was apparently expected to serve domestic as well as military purposes probably struck him as inconvenient and confusing. He may very well have felt that there was a need for more accommodation, not least for his own very large retinue, which when he went to the border in October 1380 to negotiate a truce with the Scots, numbered 2000 men – in medieval terms, a small army. And he may also have been concerned about the way that the castle's defences were ranged along the south curtain wall, with nothing in reserve should it be captured. He therefore gave Dunstanburgh a comprehensive overhaul.

To see what he did, go back down to ground level, out through the gatehouse again, and round to the right, and stand on the path by its west tower, looking towards the north. Had you been there in about 1400, you would in fact have been staring into a gateway – you can see the base of the wall to which it was attached projecting from the side of the gatehouse. And on the other side of the path you can see the foundations of a second wall. Continuing up the path, you will come to the remains of a second gatehouse, which was thus approached in the narrow space between two walls.

This second gatehouse was built by a mason named Henry Holme, with whom Duke John made a contract for its construction in July 1383. Holme was to construct a gatehouse of freestone – that is, of ashlar – which would be vaulted under the arch, and have a portcullis, a barbican, a spiral staircase, a postern and the apparatus for a bridge. The bridge was probably at the south end of the path leading to the new gatehouse. The ground there was formerly higher than it is today, with a considerable drop to the level of the ground in front of the castle; that drop was now to be spanned by a gangway which could be lifted like a drawbridge. A barbican was an outwork which projected immediately in front of the new gatehouse, in a position which meant that attackers coming up the passage-way between the two walls could have been showered with stones, spears and arrows before they could even reach the gatehouse. Walls and barbican together were intended to make the approach to the new entrance a deathtrap.

Henry Holme was an experienced mason – he had been recorded as working at Berwick as long ago as 1360 – but in spite of the order that ashlar be used, the masonry of the 1380s was not of good quality. Perhaps the new gatehouse at Dunstanburgh was built too quickly to have been built well. It was reported to be on the point of collapse as early as 1431, and today it has almost entirely disappeared. Only its foundations – complete with portcullis grooves – are still visible. And the same shortcomings affected the other buildings constructed at the same time.

Although little is left of this entrance, enough survives to show what John of Gaunt's plan for the castle was. He obviously wanted a conventional stronghold which could resist the Scots, and therefore created a self-contained inner ward – that is a courtyard surrounded by buildings – within the huge expanses of the original enclosure. To bring this into being the duke turned in the first instance to one of the most notable English architects of the later middle ages, John Lewyn of Durham. A contract drawn up on 25 October 1380 specified that Lewyn would build for John of Gaunt an ashlar 'mantlet', or surrounding wall, twenty feet high and battlemented, 'round the great tower of his castle of Dunstanburgh'. Its proposed length, just over 180 feet (54m), identifies this 'mantlet' as the wall whose foundations can still be seen, outlining the perimeter of the new inner ward.

Although the gatehouse in the west wall was the last element in John of Gaunt's programme for the castle to be completed, it seems likely that it formed part of his plans from the first, and that when Henry Holme built it, he was carrying out work originally planned by John Lewyn and the duke. An essential part of their design was that the old gatehouse should have its entrance completely blocked up, so that in future it could serve as the castle keep, entered from the new inner ward. In that capacity it could have housed John of Gaunt himself when he visited Dunstanburgh, while also providing lodgings for an enlarged garrison in times of siege, and a last line of defence if the new gatehouse was stormed.

There was to be no direct access to the inner ward from the new gatehouse, mainly for defensive reasons, but probably also to avoid congestion in the courtyard's limited space. A man on horseback passing under the new gate would thus have found himself in the corner of the outer ward,

The ruins of Dunstanburgh, as drawn by Francis Place in 1678. This drawing is particularly valuable in showing the old Gatehouse towers, and the arched gateway into John of Gaunt's gatehouse. The tower visible between them is probably the one which stood at the north-east corner of the inner ward, where its base can still be seen (British Museum)

with a wall on his right. No doubt he would have dismounted at this point, and seen his horse led away to the stables or set free to graze. Following in his footsteps, you should now walk through the gate and along what is left of the wall, until you come to the remains of a small square tower at the corner, built to command the entrance to the inner ward. Turning right and right again, through a gap once filled by another, smaller, gatehouse which Holme built in 1382 or 1383, will bring you into that ward.

Holme's contract of 1383 specified that, as well as the new gatehouse, he was to build six houses, all vaulted and with fireplaces and windows. In the foundations of the tower you can just see the base for a barrel vault of the sort that Holme undertook to erect. It is rarely possible to say much about the other buildings which completed the perimeter of the inner ward. But if you walk round in an anti-clockwise direction you will come first to the splendid oven in which the garrison's bread would

have been baked, doubtless using corn grown on the Duke of Lancaster's estates nearby and stored in the castle grange.

The building along the courtyard's west wall may have been a kitchen – it would certainly have made sense to have it there so close to the castle's water supply in its well. This well, incidentally, was worked by hand, a mid sixteenth-century report observing that 'there is no horse mill in the said castle', meaning that it had no

A fine late fourteenth-century oven in the inner ward

horse-powered mill for drawing water. And there was also a range of buildings, perhaps containing some of the houses that Holme undertook to build attached to the north-east corner of the old gatehouse. A passage through this range from the entrance to the inner ward gave access to that gatehouse's staircase and so to the chambers inside.

West Curtain and Lilburn Tower

If you now continue north along the west curtain wall, you will come to a shapeless lump of masonry, all that is left of a turret. Perhaps it was built at the same time as the second gatehouse, using the same inferior stone or the same shoddy workmanship. In 1678 it was still standing, a two-storey rectangular building with battlements at the top. Further along, however, you come to a tower which, like the first gatehouse, has

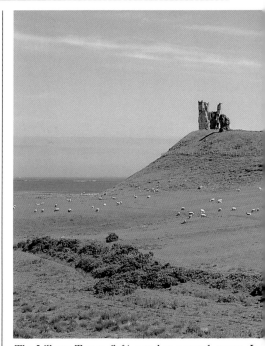

The Lilburn Tower (left) acted as a watch-tower. It

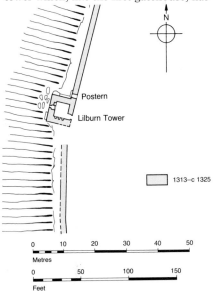

Plan of Lilburn Tower and the postern in the west curtain wall

survived much better than the later structures. It takes its name from John de Lilleburn, a retainer of Thomas of Lancaster's who managed to make his peace with Edward II after his lord's final rebellion and execution in 1322, and was appointed keeper of the castle in January 1323. He is recorded as receiving twenty marks (£13.33p) for works on the castle during that year, so he may have built the tower, or more probably, completed it.

Unlike the first gatehouse, with its curved 'drums' projecting at the front, the **Lilburn Tower** is severely rectangular. This may indicate that it was the work of another mason, though the stonework of both buildings is of the same high quality. But it probably also shows that the Lilburn Tower was intended to serve a different purpose. As often as not, curved towers were built in the early fourteenth-century for no better reason than that they

controlled the western approach to the castle

were in fashion, following the example of Edward I's great castles in Wales. But they also had the advantage that their curves could deflect and lessen the impact of missiles thrown by besiegers. Standing beside it, and looking west, over the precipitous drop to the plain below, you can see that the Lilburn Tower can never have been in serious danger of being attacked. It was principally a watch tower, with turrets at about sixty feet (18m) above the ground, and also a residence.

Its ground floor may have been a basement, the rectangular holes in its south wall being probably designed for storage, but the top two (you can tell their number from the holes for the joists which once supported the floors) would have housed some of the soldiers. Each storey seems to have consisted of a single large chamber, these being linked by a spiral staircase in the tower's south-east corner,

Lilburn Tower on the west curtain

Engraving of the Lilburn Tower in about 1870, showing the garderobe shutes still in perfect condition. The great crack in the north wall has since been repaired and the doorway unblocked (History of the Berwickshire Naturalists' Club, 6)

and they each had a fireplace as well as finely cut two-light windows. And if you look cautiously round the outside of the west wall, you can see something of the castle's sanitary arrangements, in the shape of two garderobe-shutes supported by corbels. On the north side of the tower you will notice that the walkway on the curtain wall runs *through* the tower by a door on its first floor (presumably it was the same on the other side). This meant that if the soldiers in the tower were called to arms from their lodgings, they could run straight on to the walls without having to go down to ground level and up again. Immediately to the north of the tower is a postern, with a gate secured by bars – you

can see the holes for them, two on each side. So sharp is the fall of the ground here, that it seems likely that this gate would have been used less for making raids and sallies from, than as an observation point.

Outer Ward

From the Lilburn Tower the wall continues north for a short distance and comes to an end at the edge of a hundred foot (30m) cliff. Terminating here also is the Great Whin Sill, an outcrop of dark basaltic rock which runs across Northumberland from the south-west of the county to the coast, and which provided, among other things, the strategic heights along which most of the Roman Wall was built. In the mid sixteenth-century there was said to have been a wall at this point, though nothing remains of it now. It may seem to have been unduly pessimistic to suppose that this tremendous natural defence needed any human assistance, but in fact the wall, which was only 7½ft (2.3m) high, was probably intended less to keep enemies out than to keep livestock in, by stopping them straying over the cliff.

Before you continue to walk along the curtain wall where it begins again on the east side of the headland, it is worth pausing for a moment to consider the great expanse of open ground in front of you. It was not always completely empty. In the Middle Ages there would have been a number of buildings dotted around it, probably made principally of wood but with stone foundations – the grange, barn, cattle shed and stable mentioned at various times in fourteenth- and fifteenth-century records. Dunstanburgh was the centre of a lordship, and the produce of its estates was stored here, much of it being needed to feed the garrison, which could be large. Early in 1323 when the Anglo-

Aerial photograph of Dunstanburgh Castle from the east, showing the vast extent of the outer ward unencumbered by buildings (Airfotos, Newcastle)

Scottish wars were at their height, the castle was said to have been held by thirty heavily-armed and one hundred lightly-armed horsemen, so if they were all present at once the demand for victuals, stabling and housing would have been very great.

But, except in times of emergency, the manpower placed in a medieval castle was usually quite small, being added to only as and when the needs of the moment required this. In 1400, for instance, the constable of Dunstanburgh was expected to command a force of only ten men-at-arms and twenty mounted archers. Even so, accommodating at least thirty horses can have been neither easy nor cheap. It is possible that the foundations of sheds and shacks may still exist under the grass. But since it was reported in the early eighteenth century that the area had lately been used to grow corn, is seems likely that most of such remains were ploughed up long ago.

In the Middle Ages it was important that a good deal of this outer ward, as it became, should remain unoccupied, if the castle was to fulfil what appears to have been one of its original functions, that of providing space for refugees from the countryside around when they had to flee from Scottish raiders. We can imagine smoke rising from the villages to the west, as Embleton and Rennington went up in flames, and their inhabitants pouring in with such possessions as they could carry away, and above all with their own, and their lord's, livestock – without cattle for

Egyncleugh Tower from the shore-line.
The moat can be seen on the left side.

ploughing there could be no sowing and no harvest In times of crisis, the interior of the castle must have looked like a cattle market, and the noise – and smell – would have been considerable.

If you start walking south along the remains of the east-facing curtain wall, you can see that this, too, compared with the old gate house and Lilburn Tower, was built of inferior masonry. Occasionally you may notice joins in the stonework, showing that it was built in sections, and it has been plausibly suggested that the wall was constructed by the peasantry of the local villages as one of the services they owed to their lord, with each village thus making a separate contribution to the defences. On this side of the castle high-quality masonry was not really needed, and we may guess that the work was done without much enthusiasm and consequently not very well. With the possible exception of a short stretch

towards its north end which seems to be made of solid masonry, the wall consists of no more that an earth core with a rough limestone facing on each side.

There are three garderobes in this stretch of wall, perhaps intended for the use of refugees to the castle – the garrison would probably have used those in the various towers. Dunstanburgh was in fact well supplied with privies – medieval people may never have heard of germs, but they were not so ignorant or stupid as to suppose that sanitation was unimportant, or to be unaware that their excrement was best disposed of outside a castle's walls. About halfway along the east curtain you can see, looking west, the only traces to survive of the structures which once stood in this part of the castle, a large rectangular enclosure – possibly once a vegetable garden, something quite often found in a medieval castle – with the foundations of a building at its higher end. It is not possible to say precisely what this was, but no doubt it served to store corn, hay, or some other product of the Duchy estate.

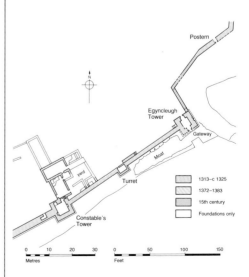

The Constable's and Egyncleugh Towers

Looking along the south curtain wall to the Constable's and Egyncleugh Towers

Egyncleugh Tower and South Curtain

As you get back towards the south-facing curtain wall – passing a postern gate giving access to the coast as you go – it becomes possible once more to appreciate the finer and more lasting qualities of the castle's stonework, although even here, where the masonry is largely that of the early fourteenth-century, time and the elements have done much to wear it away.

This is particularly true of the so-called **Egyncleugh Tower** at the wall's eastern end. Its name is mysterious. When first recorded, in the late 1450s, it was called the Elgyn Tower, perhaps after some unknown builder or restorer. A 'cleugh' or clough is a ravine, and the appropriateness of that part of the name will not be questioned by anyone who looks down into the chasm below the tower. Its exposed position has meant that the tower

has continued to crumble in relatively recent times. A sketch of 1862 shows garderobes at its north-east corner, which by 1891 had collapsed into the seas below. And its condition today is fairly ragged.

At ground level, openings to the north and south under what was once a barrel vault, made the Egyncleugh Tower a gateway. An account of 1368 refers to a 'watergate' in the castle, and no doubt this was it, giving access by drawbridge, over a moat in front, to the coastline and port to the south.

Not much is known about the port, though it seems to have been a small one, probably only a fishing harbour. It has mistakenly been said to have been large because of a belief that Henry VIII's fleet sheltered at Dunstanburgh on its way up the north-east coast in January 1514. In fact the entire 'fleet' on this occasion consisted of four ships. Only two of these vessels were recorded at Dunstanburgh,

Medieval fishermen hauling in their catch (British Museum)

and their being there had nothing to do with any port. They just happened to be near Dunstanburgh when the royal agent who was looking for these ships made contact with them.

No doubt it was in the small harbour here that Thomas of Lancaster's boat was kept – new oars were bought for it in 1320 – and also the new boat bought for the castle in 1368. But, although supplies were occasionally brought to Dunstanburgh by sea, as when a quantity of lead for buildings was carried there from Newcastle in 1443, goods are more often recorded as being transported overland in carts, and on the whole the port seems to have been a useful appendage to the castle rather than an essential part of it. Its existence within reach of a postern gate offered the possibility of escape should the castle look like falling to attack, but the fact that it was placed on the south side of the castle, that is, on the side on which enemies were most likely to be active, would have reduced its value in this respect. In the end, perhaps its most valuable function was to supply the garrison with fish for eating on Fridays, and on other days of religious abstinence.

Returning now to the Egyncleugh Tower, above the gateway there were two floors, entered by a spiral staircase set in the angle immediately west of the gateway on the north side. The layout of these floors was much like that of the Lilburn Tower, with which the Egyncleugh Tower was probably contemporary, each storey consisting of a single room with a fireplace, a garderobe, and at least one window apiece. Again, like the Lilburn Tower, the purpose of the Egyncleugh Tower may have been as much domestic, to house members of the garrison, as military. But it stood in an obviously defensive position and it is likely that here, too, there was direct access from inside the tower to the walkway along the battlements of the adjacent curtain wall, again so that the soldiers could man that wall as soon as the alarm was raised. And if the men in the Egyncleugh Tower needed reinforcing, the stairway leading up into the Tower also gave direct access to the battlements beside it.

The defences of Dunstanburgh were largely concentrated in the **south curtain wall**, the castle having been deliberately constructed from the first so that it was

Medieval castle under siege. Notice the miner hacking at the foot of the wall (British Library)

there that any attack would have to be made. The south curtain therefore held a series of towers and turrets.

After the Egyncleugh Tower you will come to the remains of a small turret, only one storey of which still stands above ground level. You can see that it juts out well ahead of the wall, as do all the defensive buildings here. This was because the greatest danger to a medieval castle was less the catapult or the battering ram, than the digging of tunnels to undermine the foundations of the walls. If miners were able to get close enough to the foot of a straight wall to start operations, the defenders could only throw spears or shoot arrows at them by standing up and leaning out, and they risked being shot themselves by other attackers. By having towers which projected in front of the walls, the garrison could attack miners from the side, while at the same time keeping safely behind their own battlements.

Rather more survives of the next building along this wall, the **Constable's Tower**. The constable was the castle's principal officer, the director of its defence in time of war, the man responsible for the maintenance and repair of its buildings, and also the overall manager of the surrounding manors, for whose inhabitants Dunstanburgh Castle must have been a mighty symbol of the local power of the Duke of Lancaster, as well as a fortress and refuge against the invasions of the Scots. The rents and agricultural produce from these manors would be kept at Dunstanburgh in the constable's custody, and so would the estate records. As befitted his importance, the constable was well-housed, as you can see from the building named from him. With its ground floor chamber and two upper storeys, his tower was a building of quality.

Looking up you can see a spiral staircase in the north-east corner leading to the first and second floors. Both these have fireplaces – nobody who has visited Dunstanburgh in winter will need to be told why the castle was so lavishly furnished with fireplaces – but their most interesting features are the south-facing windows, with double lights and window seats. The regularity of the vaults over the windows, and the crisp shaping of the seats, within the framework of regular blocks of ashlar, show the same architecturally high standards as the old gatehouse, constructed at the same time as the Constable's Tower. And at ground level the recess for storage in the east wall, the fireplace in the west wall, and the window looking back into the castle are no less well made. The fine stone floor may be original.

Attached to this tower on its north side was a complex of small buildings for the use of the constable and his household – the foundations of some of them can still be seen. It is, however, rarely possible even to guess what these structures were.

Getting dressed by the fire. A medieval illustration in the British Library

Celebration of Mass in a medieval chapel (Walters Art Gallery, Baltimore)

But their domestic nature is shown by the oven in the north-west corner of the building stretching back immediately behind the tower, which suggests both that there was a kitchen here, and that the room to the north of it was the hall (traditionally placed near the kitchen), where the constable and his retinue ate.

In fact there were more buildings in this part of the castle than can now be seen. A resistivity survey carried out by Newcastle University's Department of Physics detected foundations of walls on either side of the visible ruins. Some stood in what appears to have been a small courtyard formed by a wall running from the north-west corner of the Constable's Tower complex to the tower built by John of Gaunt at the entrance to the inner ward devised in the 1380s. To the east, the underground ruins may include those of the chapel. There certainly was one in the castle and, in about this position, its remains being said to have been still visible behind the east end of the south curtain wall in the late eighteenth century.

All medieval castles of any importance

had a chapel. That at Dunstanburgh was clearly as well kept as any of the buildings, being largely re-equipped in 1443 with a new chalice, altar-board, vestments and altar-cloths, all bought in London. There is no surviving reference to a chaplain however, and the castle must have been served by a priest from one of the nearby villages. Also somewhere under the ground lie the remains of the rooms used by the lord's officers when they came to Dunstanburgh to inspect the affairs of his Northumberland manors. In 1443, which seems to have been a busy year, his auditor and receiver stayed in the castle, and for their visit two mattresses, stuffed with wool, were bought. Perhaps, as was common in the Middle Ages, these were intended for a single large bed in which the two men lay side to side. If so, they would have had sleeping quarters of some splendour, in a bed with a cover, a canopy and three curtains. Such visitors clearly expected to eat in style, too, since two new dining tables were bought on the same occasion.

After the Constable's Tower the south curtain wall continues towards the old gatehouse, interrupted first by a garderobe and then by a small watch-tower, or perhaps a sentry post, the latter supported by corbels. There were no stairs up to it, so it could only have been entered from the walkway along the wall, which here, as elsewhere, has lost a good deal of its upper levels. Its original height, and the effect it must have had on any would-be besieger, can be deduced from the fact that the battlement-walk on the south curtain was originally joined to the old gatehouse by a door on the latter's third floor.

Later History of Dunstanburgh

The Scots are known to have raided around Dunstanburgh several times in the late fourteenth and early fifteenth-

The splendid windows of the Constable's Tower. Their quality illustrates the high architectural standards found in Thomas of Lancaster's castle

centuries, and no doubt the castle then acted as a refuge for the peasantry who suffered at the hands of the invaders, as it had done in the 1340s. But the Scots are never recorded as actually attacking the castle, which is only known to have come under siege during the Wars of the Roses. By then Dunstanburgh had long been the property of the Crown, thanks to the usurpation of the throne by John of Gaunt's son, who became Henry IV in 1399. The fact that the kings of England were now also dukes of Lancaster, with substantial properties in the region, was doubtless an important reason why the

north of England was decidedly Lancastrian in sympathy. Even after their disastrous defeat at Towton in March 1461, forces loyal to Henry VI (1422-61) were active in Northumberland, where they were helped by their possession of a number of important castles, of which Dunstanburgh was one. In December 1462, therefore, it was besieged by Yorkist troops. On this occasion its commander, Sir Ralph Percy, surrendered to Edward IV (1461-83) on condition that he was allowed to remain in control of the castle, but Percy soon betrayed the new King, and returned to his Lancastrian allegiance. Only in June 1464, after the last army loyal to Henry VI had been destroyed at the Battle of Hexham, was Dunstanburgh finally surrendered to the Earl of Warwick, then busily engaged in earning his title of the Kingmaker, who spent the feast of the Nativity of St John the Baptist (24 June) in the castle – presumably he worshipped in its chapel on a feast day of such importance.

Signature of Richard Neville (Warwick the Kingmaker) 1464 (British Library)

Dunstanburgh had been besieged, not assaulted, and in 1462 it was starvation, not bombardment, which caused the men of the garrison to surrender, after they had been reduced to eating their horses. The Yorkists, who would have found a blockade all the easier to maintain because neither now nor at any other time was Dunstanburgh equipped with guns to keep attackers at bay, wanted to keep this and the other Northumbrian castles intact, so that they could put their own men into them, not to reduce them to useless rubble. Yet after 1464 Dunstanburgh was never of military importance again. Small sums were occasionally spent on repairs during the 1460s and 1470s, but never enough to make up for the effects of wind, rain and long-term neglect, and the garrison seems to have taken to piracy, perhaps for lack of anything better to do. In one fifteenth-century lawsuit, a Breton merchant complained that he had been robbed at sea, and he and his crew 'put in a dark prison' (perhaps the cell under the western side of the old gatehouse) in Dunstanburgh Castle. After a last expenditure of some £27 on repairs in 1503 – the year of the so-called Treaty of Perpetual Peace between England and Scotland, which it was hoped would bring peace to the borders – the maintenance of the castle seems to have stopped altogether, and by the early 1520s it was serving no purpose more useful than that of a source of lead for the repair of the roof of Wark Castle on the River Tweed.

It is not surprising in the circumstances that a survey of 1538 should have described Dunstanburgh as 'a very ruinous house and of small strength', or that only the old gatehouse should have been still habitable. Over £100 would be needed to put the castle in a state of repair. It was more than Henry VIII (1509-47) was prepared to spend on it. By 1543 a few repairs had been carried out on the walls, but John of Gaunt's gatehouse had 'fallen down wholly', there was stone lying around everywhere, and the lead was being stolen daily from the roofs. England and Scotland were at war again by this time, but the constable of Dunstanburgh – who must have been living in considerable discomfort if he actually occupying the castle – compla of having the utmost difficulty in secur

Fifteenth-century siege with heavy guns,
something Dunstanburgh never had
to face (University of Jena)

now be but ramparts of chaff against our modern engines of war'.

The fabric fell more and more into ruin, becoming the preserve of the seabird and the haunt not only of the occasional tourist or tramp but also of a resident ghost, that of Sir Guy the Seeker. A highly romantic ballad told how Sir Guy, by failing to draw a magical sword at the proper moment, missed the opportunity of rescuing a beautiful lady held in an enchanted captivity in a hall under the castle, and thereafter wandered round the ruins, moaning dismally to anyone who would listen 'Could I but find the sword again'. The prospect of meeting this depressing spectre did not, in fact, prevent the castle's owners from commissioning occasional alterations and repairs. Thus

payment of his wages.

In 1550 yet another survey reported that the castle was 'in wonderful great decay' but only 72s 8d (£3.64p) was spent on repairs, and that not for another twelve years. The truth of the matter was that the castle was no longer perceived as being of any use. A report made in 1584 described Dunstanburgh as potentially 'a house of great force of strength', but conceded that it was not really needed now, even though Scottish cattle-thieves were sometimes still active in its vicinity. The Union of the Crowns of England and Scotland in 1603 made it even more redundant, and in 1604 King James I and VI (1603-25) sold it, after which the castle passed into the hands first of the Grey family and then of the Earls of Tankerville. Since it had never been equipped to resist cannon fire it played no part in the Civil Wars of the seventeenth-century. 'What is become of the Castles of Dunstinbrough, Bambrough, Alnwick and Tinmouth?' asked one writer in the 1650s before answering his own question, 'They would

Nineteenth-century romantic imagery
of knightly chivalry

the passage-way through Thomas of Lancaster's gatehouse was reshaped in the 1850s or 1860s, and further works were reported in 1898. But the costs of maintenance became too much, and in 1929 Sir Arthur Sutherland, a Newcastle shipowner who was the last of these proprietors, gave Dunstanburgh into the guardianship of H M Office of Works, a forerunner of English Heritage.

Further works of restoration followed, before the outbreak of the Second World War made Dunstanburgh, unexpectedly and presumably for the last time, the scene of military activity. In 1940 the need to protect the north-east coast against possible invasion led to a small Royal Armoured Corps detachment installing itself among the ruins, and to a gunpit being dug outside the walls. But although mines were laid along the shore the soldiers were soon withdrawn, and

Castle ruin with Jackdaw and Magpie. A woodcut by Thomas Bewick

Dunstanburgh Castle, which had been so seldom disturbed since the sixteenth century, was once more left to the Fulmar, the Cormorant and the Kittiwake.

Bibliography

E. Bateson (ed.), *Northumberland County History* Vol. II (Newcastle upon Tyne, 1895)

C. H. Hartshorne, *Feudal and Military Antiquities of Northumberland* (London, 1858)

M.Hislop, *'John of Gaunt's building works at Dunstanburgh Castle'*, in *Archaeologia Aeliana* 5th series Vol 23 (1995) pp.139-44

J. R. Maddicott, *Thomas of Lancaster 1307-1322* (Oxford, 1970)

M. Prestwich, English Castles in the reign of Edward II, in *Journal of Medieval History* Vol. 8 (1982) pp.159-178

W. D. Simpson, Dunstanburgh Castle, in *Archaeologia Aeliana* 4th Series Vol. 16 (1939) pp.31-42

W. D. Simpson, Further Notes on Dunstanburgh Castle, in *Archaeologia Aeliana* 4th Series Vol. 27 (1949) pp.1-28

Biographical Notes

Thomas of Lancaster (c1278-1322)

Thomas Earl of Lancaster, the first builder of Dunstanburgh, was the nephew of Edward I and the cousin of Edward II. The lord of five earldoms, he was easily the greatest subject in the realm, and his wealth and the lavishness with which he used it, can both be deduced from the splendour of the ruins at Dunstanburgh. Unfortunately, the Earl was also a useless and repulsive person (much like his royal cousin), who proved unable to get on with his king, his wife, his fellow barons and his own retainers, many of whom deserted

Fourteenth-century pilgrim badge showing scenes from the life of Thomas of Lancaster. In the bottom right he is being beheaded (British Museum)

him when, after many years of largely unconstructive opposition to royal policies, he tried to lead a rebellion against Edward II in 1322. On that occasion he and his remaining followers decided, after much dithering, to retreat to Dunstanburgh – once there, they could have remained in touch with the Scots, with whom they were by now in treasonable correspondence. But they were intercepted by forces loyal to the King and defeated at Boroughbridge in Yorkshire. Lancaster was captured, given a summary trial, and on 22 March executed as a traitor, having first been exposed to the insults of a crowd which mocked him and pelted him with snowballs. Later attempts to have him proclaimed a saint were entirely due to his political opposition to a deservedly unpopular monarch, and owed nothing to his personal qualities, which seem to have been thoroughly disagreeable.

John of Gaunt (1340-99)

The third son of Edward III, John of Gaunt (so called because he was born at Ghent in Belgium) was a leading figure in English political life for some thirty years, owing his great influence to his birth and his enormous wealth – he was so rich that he had a category specially reserved for him in the carefully graduated poll tax of 1379, and paid more than anyone else in England. He was especially prominent in the 1370s during his father's declining years and at the beginning of the reign of Richard II (1377-99), who was only eleven years old when he became king. This was a time of strain and difficulty; the war with

France was going badly, while taxation was high to pay for it, and John of Gaunt was widely blamed for the government's failures. His reputation suffered from his association with Katherine Swinford, his mistress who eventually became his third wife, and he was also suspected of wishing to play the part of a wicked uncle to his young nephew. As a result, he came to be greatly hated, and was lucky to be in the north when the Peasants' Revolt broke out in 1381 (he may have visited Dunstanburgh in this year). His first wife Blanche, through whom he became Duke of Lancaster and lord of Dunstanburgh, died of plague in 1369, and he subsequently married Constance, daughter of Pedro the Cruel of Castile, devoting his time and resources in the 1380s principally to efforts to make himself King of Castile in the right of his wife. But the best he could achieve was the marriage of his daughter to the heir to the Castilian throne. He had a wide experience as a soldier, as his alterations to Dunstanburgh show, but on the whole he was more energetic than successful in military

John of Gaunt (1340-99), as depicted on his own great seal. A cast in the Society of Antiquaries of London

matters. Conventional in his attitudes, and probably little more than mediocre in his abilities, the fears that he would try to usurp the throne were certainly unjustified; he was loyal to his father and nephew, and in his later years became an important force for stability in England.

Glossary

Ashlar Rectangular hewn blocks of stone laid in regular courses with fine vertical joints

Barbican Outward extension of a gateway protecting the entrance from attack

Barrel Vault Vault with semi-cylindrical roof

Corbel Stone or wooden projection from a wall acting as a bracket to support a beam or other weight

Curtain Wall Defensive wall enclosing a courtyard

Forebuilding Defensive structure protecting the entrance to a keep or other building

Freestone Building stone which is fine-grained and can be worked in any direction

Garderobe Latrine or privy

Keep Main tower of a castle, forming the centre of its defences

Loophole Narrow vertical slit in a wall, which let a little light in, while allowing the defenders to shoot out with arrows and crossbow bolts

Mantlet A surrounding wall, often a screen of masonry for other walls or defences

Portcullis Iron-shod wooden grille, suspended by chains in grooves in front of a gate or door and lowered to ground level for additional security

Postern Secondary small entrance or gateway in a wall, often concealed and normally behind or to the side of a building

Resisstivity Resistance to the flow of electricity through soil can be measured. A survey can map buried features which hold more moisture than solid features.

Rib Projecting band of stone structurally supporting a vaulted roof

Vault Arched roof or ceiling, often supported by stone ribs

Ward Courtyard of a castle